SOCIOLOGY
AND
PASTORAL CARE

Francois Houtart

SOCIOLOGY
AND
PASTORAL CARE

Translated from the French
by
MALACHY CARROLL

Franciscan Herald Press
Chicago, Illinois 60609

SOCIOLOGY AND PASTORAL CARE, by Francois Houtart, translated by Malachy Carroll from the French work, *Sociologie et Pastorale,* published by Editions Fleurus, Paris, France. Library of Congress Catalog Card Number: 65-25839. Copyright 1965 by Franciscan Herald Press, 1434 West 51st Street, Chicago, Illinois 60609. Designed by Publication Associates. Made in the United States of America.

IMPRIMI POTEST: Dominic Limacher O.F.M., *Minister Provincial;* NIHIL OBSTAT: Mark Hegener O.F.M., *Censor Deputatus;* IMPRIMATUR: Most Rev. Cletus F. O'Donnell, D.D., *Vicar General, Archdiocese of Chicago.* August 29, 1965.

PREFACE

VATICAN II *provides a clear indication that the Church is pre-occupied with the problems of a world in the throes of change. The pastoral adaptations now in progress show a new perception of the inexhaustible riches of the evangelical message. They are also the expression of the presence of the Church in the ways of men, who are now involved in one of the most fundamental mutations of their entire history.*

There has been much talk about "shared pastoral work," and the term is even in danger of becoming modish. Still, it does point decidedly to the movement in progress and the direction to be taken. Pastoral care is no longer simply the fruit of an individual action, however dedicated and spiritual. In a world whose socialization has been underlined by the encyclical Mater et magistra, *new forms of apostolic action have come into being. They imply enlarged dimensions, and an increasingly vigorous pastoral specialization which demands more intensive collaboration and a re-definition of roles, especially of those of the priest, the nun and the laity.*

This complexity of pastoral tasks implies a gradual formulation of pastoral plans. If this is urgent at the local parish level, it is much more so in the case of a large town or city, a region,

v

a diocese, a nation and a continent. This book by Canon Houtart takes an immediate universal viewpoint, for it shows that these problems, far from being peculiar to a geographical region or to a particular culture, are today facing everyone and must be solved collectively.

However, the pastoral plans, the re-definition of roles, the transformation of institutions, cannot be carried out without using certain techniques. Mere good will and the authority conferred by hierarchic rank are no longer sufficient. Competence is also needed.

Side by side with psychology and the organizational sciences, in the development of the techniques necessary for such a task, sociology has its place as a discipline whose object is the knowledge of social facts, both lay and religious. It is based on permanent and systematic information concerning the evolution of such facts, and in particular on statistical equipment.

All this may seem very remote from pastoral concerns, and one might even be inclined to regard it as in conflict with the work of the Holy Spirit in souls. However, this would be to misunderstand pastoral care and to miss the point that the role of human sciences makes them the auxiliaries of this care. One of the merits of the present book is that it meets and answers this objection. In his redemptive plan, God has willed to use us as the instrument of his work, but he expects from us a collaboration of our whole being, of our will and of our intelligence.

Let us hope that the bridge may be more and more solidly established between the sociologists and the pastors, so that, through the constant improvement of their hypotheses and their methods, the sociologists may be able to appreciate more and more clearly the needs of the pastors, and that those responsible for pastoral care may face up more and more wholeheartedly to the collective dimension of their mission.

L. J. Cardinal Suenens

CONTENTS

INTRODUCTION

1. PASTORAL CARE

At the present time, pastoral care is the subject of courses and of numerous books and articles. However, even a cursory inspection of these writings very soon uncovers a certain confusion about the meaning to be given to this term. There is general agreement in defining it as "the action of the Church," but the word "action" is variously interpreted. Some take it in the broad sense to include the whole body of ecclesial action; while others limit its application either to the governing functions of the Church or to other particular aspects of the Church's action, such as catechesis, liturgy, mission, and so forth.

It is beyond our purpose here to attempt an assessment of these various opinions. Such an undertaking is the province of theology, and demands specialized investigations and systematic treatment, this being fully justified, moreover, by the importance of the whole question.

However, to establish the viewpoint we take when we speak of pastoral care, we shall adopt the definition given by Father Dingemans O.P. — a definition he himself qualifies as provisional: "Pastoral care is the action of the Church by which, under

3

the guidance of the Holy Ghost, she visibly carries out the mission entrusted to her by Christ, and labors to complete the Father's plan for the salvation of mankind."[1]

We emphasize, in the first place, that pastoral care is taken here in its broad sense. It includes the whole activity which the Church uses in the exercise of her specific mission. It therefore excludes the pursuit of aims which are in no way connected with that mission, or have only an accidental and tenuous connection with it.

Furthermore, since responsibility for the Church has been entrusted to the Hierarchy, pastoral care, as the name already indicates, is primarily the activity of the pastors and of those who directly participate in their priesthood. However, as Canon Dondeyne underlines, the Christian becomes, through baptism and faith, a member of the apostolic community and enters into God's plans for the world. Membership of the Church of Christ is at once a grace and a responsibility, and every Christian has a duty to collaborate in building up, in "edifying" the Church, the word "edify" being taken in its twofold sense.[2] In its liaison with the Hierarchy, every lay apostolate derives, therefore, from pastoral work, and is included in that work.

The whole matter resolves itself, therefore, into a search for the forms best calculated to secure the fulfilment of the mission which Christ entrusted to the Church: *"Go to all nations . . . Teach . . . Baptize . . . You will be witnesses unto me . . ."*
"Go . . ."

In the circumstances of today, this missionary command takes on a very special resonance. It does so, on the one hand, because the growth of our technological civilization, with all the problems incident to that growth, has assumed cosmic dimensions; and, on the other hand, because the Church is faced with the

4

need to be a missionary Church, taking the term literally, in every continent, whether it is a question of christianizing a pagan people or of rechristianizing a people whose Christianity has become moribund.

... *"to all nations . . ."*

To go to all nations means going to that huge mass of three thousand million people only eighteen per cent of whom are Catholics. This simple proportion (18:100) is sufficient of itself to show the extent of the work to be done, and quite clearly, in the years to come, the Church will be faced with a task of evangelization much more complex still. Demographic studies predict a doubling of world population by the end of the century, and this in continents where society and culture are in full evolution and where an essentially dynamic pastoral approach is therefore demanded.

"Teach . . ."

By definition, to teach means to transmit knowledge to others. The primary object of the minister of the Church is, therefore, the transmission of the Gospel message. In other words, it is the proclamation of the Redemption by Christ, the Son of God, and the proclamation of the Love of the Father; the message of hope concerning the Kingdom; the communication of the ways which will make possible the gradual building up of children of God through Christ and through his Church.

But teaching is also the whole art of making things understood and accepted. We know, of course, that faith is a grace that cannot be circumscribed by human action. However, God has willed that men should be the instruments of its communication; and this, in turn, implies that the Church must use language and modes of transmission capable of being understood by those to whom she addresses herself. It is here that the whole problem of adaptation comes in. "The indispensability of adaptation is more than ever acute in modern times, because we have experienced changes within a few years unparalleled by any previous changes extending over several centuries. This is a fact that cannot fail to have its repercussion on the way we envisage the presentation of the Christian message."[3]

For this adaptation to be effective, account must be taken of the different socio-cultural environments which now coexist, and an effort made to discover their mental outlook, as well as the transmission channels for the values peculiar to them. It is indeed a fact that the catechetical and other methods which would succeed among Western peoples, might well fail if applied in other types of society, because of the difference in mental habits, or because these methods cannot be effectively used owing to the existence of a totally inadequate level of technical or cultural development.

". . . Baptize . . ."

Baptism is the exterior sign of a fundamental spiritual reality. If signifies incorporation in the Mystical Body, through Faith, Hope and Charity. By reason of the consequences it involves, this incorporation should be conscious and intelligent. Now, it must be admitted that this sense of belonging to the Church, of being a living member of the Mystical Body, has become very pale with many Christians, and is limited to certain steps taken at the "big moments" of life. It is important, therefore, that the Church should direct its activity towards reawakening in Christians the sense of "being the Church." This can be achieved by a better doctrinal formation, but also "by an immense effort to re-think the whole style of the celebration (of the Liturgy), to reconcile the need for popular expression with the hieratic quality of the liturgy, and to give to the faithful, within the framework of the existing discipline, every possible means of getting to understand the rites and the prayers. The liturgy, therefore, presents an urgent need for catechesis, for spiritual formation, to be pursued in all sorts of ways."[4]

"You will be witnesses unto me . . ."

The Church's activity is also a witness. While it is true that the Gospel message implies a teaching which demands an adherence through faith, it is equally true that the establishment of the Kingdom constitutes a permanent event which presupposes a participation of the whole personality. The pluralist societies in which we live are characterized, not only by the coexistence of different ideologies, but also by their omnipresence; and in such societies, the witness of the Church takes on the greatest importance. "The vast majority of people do not ask themselves whether Christianity is of divine origin, until they have sensed that origin by seeing its fruits. The fundamental missionary and apologetic problem is not so much to justify faith, as to provoke individuals and groups to inquire about it because they have personally observed its effects on the conduct of its adherents."[5] The witness of individuals is required, but also the witness of Catholic institutions not directly pastoral, such as schools, social works, and so forth.

It is indisputable that the form, even purely pastoral, of the Christian community has intrinsic aspects disserviceable to the mission. It is important, therefore, that such aspects should be reduced to a minimum, on pain of creating, within a pluralist world, a new "curtain" which would bring into coexistence two worlds at once copenetrating and impenetrable, that of the Christians and that of "the others."

While it is clear that the Church's action should adapt itself to the requirements of existing types of society, it is equally clear that the increasing complexity of these types makes pastoral care more difficult. In stable and traditional types of society, observation and personal contact were sufficient to assess the behavior patterns and mental attitudes of the group. But simple observation is today no longer sufficient. The analysis of modern types of society — think of the urban mileau, for example — demands specialized techniques of "the human sciences": sociology, psychology, ethnology, etc. Their contribution can be a very useful help to both pastors and theologians. That is why, within the Church, specialists in these diciplines are playing an increasing role. Our purpose in this book is to show what sociology can achieve in this context.

2. THE CONTRIBUTION OF SOCIOLOGY

Sociology[6] leads to a better knowledge of mankind. The source of its value is, firstly, that it presents an organized body of ideas illuminating social facts, and, secondly, that it provides an explanation of the social processes by which groups are formed, and of the major constant factors of social life. If in a given region, a rural-type society changes into an urban-type, it is not enough simply to describe this transformation. One must also attempt to determine clearly the processes of this change, to isolate the determining factors, and to predict the effects on, for example, the basic institutions of social life: the family, education, political organization — or on a religious institution such as the parish, etc.

Penetrating deeper, one must also try to discover what were the cultural values which helped to determine a particular change. Social life is not exclusively composed of factors of a mechanical type, as is the case with physics, for example, where an external influence is sufficient to modify the automatism of the variations registered by natural elements. In social life, this element

8

is internal: it concerns *man*. In the case of a transformation of a social kind, such as the change of a rural society into an urban one, economic and technical factors play a predominant part. But basic to these, there is always a cultural human factor, founded upon values. In other words, the reason why a particular economic or technical factor comes effectively into play, is that men have thought it important and useful to set it in motion. It is not by chance that scientific discoveries and their application were made within one particular culture rather than within another.

The very great similarity among social processes make it possible to establish certain generalizations, and to predict, for example, what will happen to the familial or religious set-up in a society which alters from the integrated rural type to the specialized urban type. As in every practical science, numerous observations must precede such generalizations. On the other hand, close reasoning and the elaboration of solid working hypotheses are more necessary than in other sciences, since the possibilities for experimentation are much more limited. One can detonate atomic charges in order to study their consequences, but so far no one has built a city to order for purposes of study. In sociology, comparative observation most often supplies for experimentation. One can get to know Society only by comparing types of society. International experience is as important to the sociologist, and in general to anyone who would understand society, as the laboratory is to the chemist. For, though one does not build experimental cities, the different types of existing cities are sufficiently numerous to supply diverse fields of observation.

Sociology studies, therefore, the social system which evolve according to period and place. Such systems depend on factors such as the technological level of the types of society and their geographical location (climate, altitude, etc.), and also on the values developed in the social life of the particular society. The objcct of sociology may be divided into two major components: *the social structure* and *the culture* of any group or groups being investigated.

In the first, one studies *the constitutive elements of a society,* i.e. the response to the fundamental needs of group life: the element of group continuity (the family), the social adjustment of new members (education), the organization of the group (politics), the subsistence system (economy), the pattern of leisure and the religious structure.

The second component is not concerned with these constitutive elements, but with the activity of a society, *with the way it functions,* with the manner in which the elements are inter-related. The word "culture" is taken in a much wider sense than it usually carries. It covers the behavior-patterns in social life, so as to define the social roles and the types of institutions orga-nized in answer to the fundamental needs of the group life. Thus, the social behavior-patterns of a peasant will differ widely from those of a city-dweller, whether the latter lives in London or Mexico, in Rome or in Chicago. Again, the familial roles are allotted after a very different fashion in a family of the patri-archal type and in an urban family consisting only of parents and children. Finally, the social institutions, the economic system, and even the religious institution of a village, differ radically from those of a great city. In the village set-up, certain basic institutions, such as the family and the parish, can fulfil a quasi-universal function;[7] whereas, in that of the great city, many specialized institutions are required to provide the answer to social and religious needs.

Clearly, the culture is closely dependent on the accepted values. The scale of values undoubtedly governs the role played by the culture in the whole social system; in particular, it will serve as the basic criterion, not only of the social behavior of individuals, but also when there is question of deciding the relative importance of the social roles and institutions. In a theocratic society, the priest plays a key role; in a capitalist society, the economic institution is preponderant; in a communist system, the institutional organ of the working and peasant class, the communist party, monopolizes all the roles. From the very outset, there is a scale of values.

Though we may seem to have wandered from our subject of pastoral care, we were keeping it in sight; in fact, we were preparing to get to closer grips with it. All religion is inserted into the social system, both as one of the institutions having a more or less decided importance (and therefore in contact with the other institutions of the society—the family, education, political life, economic life, leisure), and as an institution which should exercise an influence on the scale of social values. Sociology is not concerned with the influence of religion on the individual as such, or *a fortiori* with its supernatural aspect, but rather with the influence it can exercise on the social behavior of individuals. It is also concerned with religion as a social institution—i.e. as a sect or Church—in so far as it originates roles of religious significance but with a social import: the priest, the prophet, and today the militant Catholic Actionist, the deacon . . .; and finally, in so far as it creates institutes proper to it, such as the Roman Curiae, dioceses, parishes, Religious Orders, Catholic Action and the whole system of communications which these institutions establish among themselves.

11

Sociology and Pastoral Care

NOTES TO INTRODUCTION

[1]   L. Dingemans, "La Pastorale et ses buts généraux," in *ÉVANGE-LISES*, 17ᵉ année, no. 99, Nov.-Dec. 1962, p. 247.

[2]   Dondeyne, "Fondements théologique du lais" in *Éxchanges,* June 1954, p. 10.

[3]   Cardinal Marcella, "Problèmes modernes de Pastorale," in *Pastorale d' aujourdui,* Éd. du Cep, Brussels, 1962, p.20.

[4]   Canon Martimot, "La Pastorale dans le domaine liturgique," in *Pastorale d' aujourdui.*

[5]   L. Dingemans, *art. cit.* It is in this sense that we now use the term "pre-evangelization."

[6]   Among the most readily available and useful books on general sociology, there are J. H. Fichter, S.J.: *Sociology,* University of Chicago Press, Chicago, 1957; J. Leclercq: *Introduction à la sociologie,* Nauwelaerts, Louvain. — See also F. Houtart, "La Sociologie au service de la Pastorale," in *Pastorale d'aujourdui, op.cit.,* the essentials of which are in the present book.

[7]   See especially J. Laloux, *Problèmes actuels du monde rural,* la Pensée catholique, Brussels, 1957.

1.
PASTORAL CARE
AND
TECHNOLOGICAL CIVILIZATION

WHAT does sociology teach us about present-day societies? That is the question we shall now attempt to answer. Let us say here and now that we do not intend to limit our analysis to Western-type societies. The time for particularism has passed; if the Church wishes to solve the problems facing her, she must see them in a much wider perspective.[1]

The great event of our era is the unification of our planet. Indeed, the term "planetarization" is coming into current usage, because it represents a basic reality.

More and more, man lives in a world dimension, thanks no doubt to the suppression of geographic distances, but also and especially thanks to the achievements in telecommunications, which give millions of people the opportunity to discern one another more clearly. A better knowledge of others and of their situation, the increased possibilities for dialogue and encounter, open the way, not only to a rapprochement of cultures, but also to a real appreciation of the economic and social inequalities which divide nations, and which are at the root of the majority of present international problems.

15

The most obvious result of all this is that ideological isolation belongs to the past. On the one hand, there will be fewer and fewer of the preserved cultural islets whose conservatism must be assured, and, on the other hand, since events anywhere are immediately known throughout the whole world, every region has an ecumenical responsibility. That is why it is important that Christians should not remain aloof from these preoccupations, and that they should fully appreciate the role they have to play, both as men and as Christians. Are they not the bearers of a message to be passed on to others? Should they not be "the light of the world" and "the salt of the earth"?

To work for such an end is a fundamental duty imposed on modern Christians. Even more emphatically is it a fundamental duty for those whose whole activity is concerned with orientating men's minds, and with seeing that the temporal values are impregnated with these ideas.

It was this which the Holy Father stressed in his opening discourse to the Council Fathers: "Here, then, is the purpose of the Second Ecumenical Vatican Council. By uniting the major forces of the Church and by endeavoring to secure that the message of salvation may be more favorably received by mankind, it in some sort prepares for and smoothes the way leading to the unity of the human race, a unity indispensably required if the earthly city is to be made in the image of the heavenly city."[2]

This text stresses the importance, for the realization of God's plan, of the utimate objective aimed at by the work of civilization, i.e. "the unity of the human race." It clearly shows why the Church has not remained indifferent towards the wonderful inventions of human genius, towards the scientific achievements whose fruits we enjoy today, and also why "she has not failed to esteem them at their just value. Nothing that is human is foreign to the Church, because the building up of the Body of Christ, the center of history and of life, is at stake."[3]

Basic, therefore, to all our thinking about present problems of pastoral care is the fact of a fundamental mutation of mankind. All the data of the physical world in which we live, the whole organization of life in society, interhuman relations, systems of communication, and even the way man regards his "universe" and himself, are in full mutation. We are witnessing the birth of a technological civilization, and this event has consequences for the world and for the Church. We have entered upon an era wherein change is becoming a fundamental situation, and adaptation to change a basic value.

We shall first of all describe, in its broad outlines, this mutation process.

1. THE FACT

The term "mutation" immediately suggests one of the basic concepts of Darwinism. It was later adopted by the social sciences to express the idea of *"social change."*

If, then, we speak about "the mutation of mankind," we do so because we regard all the problems of the modern world — whether of the demographic, economic, philosophical, or even religious order— as being, in fact, corollaries of a fundamental problem which presents itself essentially in terms of the global change of societies and cultures.

Of course, there is nothing new about the phenomenon itself of social mutation: history has seen the displacing of certain types of society by other types. Was not the Renaissance, for instance, a period of mutation for the European society of its time?

However, there is a new and fundamental factor. Rapid social

17

change has now become a constant condition of modern societies, and this necessarily implies that men are securing for themselves the means of continual adaptation. Furthermore, a second characteristic of the phenomenon is the breadth it has assumed, both as regards its spatial dimensions and the acuteness of the situations to which it has given rise.

Before going on to analyze this process of change, we should like to clarify the viewpoint we are taking up.

To be properly understood, social change must be considered within a progressive whole. In other words, it is not sufficient merely to describe the present situations. A positive and realistic knowledge of these situations is possible only on condition that they are grasped in all their dynamism, that is, in a vision at once historical and prospective.

The Western World

In recent centuries, it was the Western World, represented at first by Europe, which underwent the most rapid process of development.

The phenomenon was essentially of cultural origin. The control of the forces of nature by the application of technological knowledge is, in effect, the result of a gradual growth of the experimental sciences, leading to a recognition of the real existence of matter and to a restructuration of the system of ideas. A civilization which placed such value on positive facts and on the application of sciences in daily life, inevitably set up a development of techniques and of their application in all areas of human life, beginning with the economic domain (industrialization, marketing, etc.).

This development overthrew the structural and cultural systems of society. Urbanization made rapid strides. Its force of

18

attraction, in conjunction with a lack of integrating elements, engendered all the classic problems of dislocation. New social stratifications appeared (the birth of a secondary and tertiary proletariat); political structures were modified. On the plane of values, the upheaval was fundamental.[4]

If our technological world is the product of certain values, in its turn it too engenders values, developing precise attitudes and even going the length of transforming the empiric foundations of metaphysical thought, of human philosophy, of man's way of regarding his world. The technological revolution has transformed and continues to modify the social systems not only, and with very sudden mutations, in countries which are only beginning to develop, but also in western and communist countries. It acts both on the organization of societies and on their system of values.

The rapidity of this upheaval creates a difficulty of adaptation which men are often insufficiently equipped to meet. They are again faced with the task of mastering anew a world which eludes them. They are obliged to re-define themselves, and to isolate what remains immutable in the constantly changing situations of their existence.

When Max Planck developed his quantum theory according to which the laws of physics do not formulate what precise changes will occur but what is likely to happen to the individuals forming part of a large group; and when Einstein showed that matter and energy are not distinct concepts but different states of the same reality considered within a relative and no longer absolute time, the vision of the world changed, and a new era began which rapidly led to the atomic and cosmic age into which we have only just entered.

Since the beginnings of what has been called the technological

19

civilization of the twentieth century, numerous social transformations have occurred. First, there is the demographic development — due to medical techniques and to the science of hygiene — which, of itself, effects considerable changes in social life.

Another fundamental effect is the ever-increasing specialization of social functions. Whatever the function in question, be it educative, economic, political, cultural, or religious, all have felt this irreversible process, which is simultaneously the effect and the cause of technological evolutions.

But, far from being completed, the process is gaining momentum. The exercise of the functions of society is becoming yet more specialized, and the social groups are coming to be still further diversified within the interior itself of the social classes.

The process may be essentially defined as the changing from a sacral society to a profane society. The words "sacral" and "profane" are here used, however, without religious associations. The domain of what is "sacred" — i.e. unchangeable, immutable, untouchable — is gradually being diminished to give place to the growing area of the relative, the transitory, the "changeable." Social cultural and economic systems, scientific theories, social structures, roles and relationhips, are undergoing rapid and profound modifications. In the majority of these cases, swiftness of adaptation has become a condition itself of human progress. Thus, tradition, age, stability, continuity, intransigence, can no longer be the fundamental social values of society. They must be replaced by other values such as innovation, youth, adaptation, mobility, tolerance.

If we are to make an assessment, it is clear that we will also note an enormous confusion, because of the difficulty experienced in working out this mutation. Some grow intoxicated with the new powers providing a new vision of man, and they make them the absolute norm. "The spaceman is neither God nor saint, but he is the first real all-mighty person who has gone up so high," sang the Soviet poets, Dykovickny and Sioboldskoi, celebrating Gargarin's achievement. Others have come to accept only a pragmatic philosophy, devoid of any reflection on man himself or on the meaning of human life and human destiny, and they make technique an end in itself. Yet others, devoting themselves courageously to metaphysical reflection, have ended by denying any meaning to human existence, and declare it to be absurd. Here we have the dramatic and admirable efforts of a humanity in quest of itself, in an era of intense mutation.

Religious values are also undergoing a profound crisis, for do they not seem bound up with all that "sacred" pattern which is in course of complete disappearance? Communist régimes regard them as obsolescent values, doomed sooner or later to disappear of their own accord. Now, at a time when we are witnessing a democratization of atheism — I speak as a sociologist — we notice the simultaneous development of a religious life much more disengaged from the traditional social forms, and of a type of religious adherence which is less and less sociological.

The Third World

Colonial expansion from Europe suddenly introduced elements of this technological civilization into the majority of African and Asiatic countries.[5] In Latin America, this penetration does not follow the same pattern, for there it results rather from a maintenance of the colonial system of dependence upon the industrial nations.

As a result of this sudden implantation of Western civilization into all the countries of the third world, the process of social change has become universal. For, while it is true that the obligation to progress has become the condition *sine qua non* of development, it is undeniable that, before they attained to this stage, all these countries have passed through a crisis of growth, more or less acute in proportion to the development of the prior traditional society. This crisis follows stages traceable in all the processes of mutation in developing countries.

It is characterized, first of all, by a period of *cultural confrontation.*

There is no doubt that the purpose pursued by the colonizing countries were essentially political and economic. Conscious of the superiority of their own technical civilization, they implanted it without the least regard for the social cultures and structures they were thus dislocating. The colonial régime inevitably suppressed the political structures. From the economic viewpoint, the clash came between an economy of subsistence and a mercantile economy. New social classes were superimposed on the old structures.

This change also affected the cultures. If the cultural values are to continue to provide a coherent explanation of the world and of criteria of behavior and action suited to a traditional society, then they must necessarily develop with the structure-changes of that society.

But clearly, too, when change intervenes, the passage from one system to another does not occur smoothly. Indeed, the gradual disintegration of the traditional values is the root cause of the painful transitional situations. In fact, the crisis of growth in a developing country is perhaps, most of all, a crisis of values; and this crisis will be more or less severe in proportion to the coherence and root grip of the system of traditional values.

Together with this cultural confrontation, the introduction of a technological civilization inevitably provokes *a break with the past,* and therefore leads to the emergence of dualist societies.

22

Situations of imbalance are created through this partial break, which occurs without a corresponding reintegration in a new system.

— *Demographic imbalance*

The introduction of medical techniques and the progressive improvement of health conditions, have led to a reduction in the death rate, particularly as regards infant mortality, without any parallel reduction in the birth rate.

The demographic explosion which results from this appears, therefore, to be one of the outcomes of the introduction of techniques without a preparatory development in the global system of values. This is what is known as the cultural lag.

As a study published by UNESCO has shown, high fecundity is strongly influenced by religious values (ancestor cult, belief in the curse of the gods), by economic reasons (a large number of children is a sign of prosperity and provides the necessary labor force in a familial economy), and by particular matrimonial customs. Such values persist for a long time; and yet, as A. Sauvy says, "a lowering of the birthrate necessitates a conscious modification of the creative process." That is why it must not be expected to diminish for at least a generation. Clearly, the education of the young can have a powerful effect in this domain.

This population growth often entails a regular and increasing impoverishment of the native peoples, owing to the fact that it is not accompanied by a growth in wealth. Now, a lowering of the birth rate means also a raising of the standards of living. This vicious circle cannot be broken without action of an international scope.

— *Economic imbalance*

If the phenomenon of pauperization derives from demographic imbalance, it equally originates in economic imbalance. The economy of the underdeveloped countries is essentially dualist. It was created, not in terms of local needs, but in terms of the profits which the colonizing centers could derive from it. Even today, it remains fundamentally dependent on the industrial powers. The colonial system developed an incomplete economy; in other words, it has excessively developed the primary sector, agriculture, and exploited the mineral wealth which should have served as a reservoir of basic resources. The system of single-crop cultivation which it established makes these economies especially vulnerable to price fluctuations on world markets. The imbalance thus created among the sectors of production, provokes a bad distribution and utilization of revenue: profits and savings, the privilege of a social class, are sent abroad and remain unproductive because they represent money gone out of effective circulation. This is one of the reasons for the absence of the investments so necessary for development (means of transport, production of energy, urban infrastructures, etc.).

On the other hand, the maintenance of a subsistence economy in rural regions, raises the whole problem of structures which are not adapted to an intensive production. The small size of land holdings, the impoverished condition of the soil, the primitive techniques of exploitation, register in many domains, as witness the undernourishment of populations which have become too numerous, and the mass exodus of the young to the urban centers where there is no employment for them and where they form a sub-proletariat. Among these non-adapted structures, we should like to emphasize the acuteness of those which lead to malnutrition. These affect more than half of mankind, and injure the individual in his health, in his capacity for work, in his spiritual life ...

The underdeveloped countries also suffer from social imbalance. At present, feudal-type or archaic societies coexist with islets of modernism, without any symbiosis existing between them.

In rural regions, patriarchal or tribal structures are often maintained within confined and closed economic areas inadequately integrated with the nation. These structures make political amalgamation and administrative centralization difficult. In many countries, the agrarian problem also exists. A reduced class of big landowners draws its prestige and its revenues from a huge mass of peasants, whom they often condemn to live in sub-human conditions, and whom they are able to exploit thanks to a métayage system in which usury is not unknown. (The métayage system is the cultivation of land for a proprietor who is paid with a part of the produce. As it was never practised in England, there is no English name for it, the French term being regularly used. In the U.S.A., where it exists in various forms, it is known as "sharecropping"—Translator).

Generally speaking, these populations have remained relegated to the margin of all civilization. Will such a state of affairs continue for long? Clearly, the spread of the means of communication has made them gradually aware of their situation.

On the other hand, urban structures are developing excessively. Because of the demographic growth, great numbers are being and will continue to be drawn towards the urban centers, where the secondary sector is usually poorly developed. This influx tends to settle together in slum areas where they form a sub-proletariat of unemployed or of casual laborers.

In Africa, the absence of "security" in the urban and industrial milieux keeps the majority of workers in a migrant condition. Negro workers do not settle down in a new working class,

25

but remain linked up with the traditional milieu. This phenomenon accounts for the migratory movements of workers, movements which in certain regions affect more than 50% of male adults. Since there is no question of their family accompanying them when these workers move from place to place, one can see the problems of social disintegration raised by this situation.

In Latin America, the urban middle class is finding great difficulty in maintaining itself. Society is developing there on the model of the social structure of the industrial type. The middle sector is plethoric, and this makes all social ascension very difficult. As for the working class which is developing in certain countries conjointly with industrialization, it has not yet found its true integration in the social system, because of its marginality or because of the social conditions imposed on it by an autochthonous North American or European capitalism.

— *Cultural imbalance*

Imbalance shows itself not merely at the level of structures. In the under-developed countries, contact with Western civilization provokes a cultural rift. These peoples no longer belong entirely to their original civilization, but they are not integrated in the Western type. "They want to be independent, that is to say, different; but they want to be modern, that is like the Westerns. The African lives in the stone age with his mother, in the middle ages with his father, and in the twentieth century in his profession. The Indian rejects the technological civilization of the West, but is nevertheless prepared to have the benefits of modern medicine, an attitude which shows a way of accepting in detail what is refused as a whole."[6]

A rift of this kind is at the root of the instability (on the

26

political plane, among others) which characterizes the majority of these countries.

Inevitably, a re-structuration on new bases meets with opposition. Such opposition is not mainly of a technical kind, but arises from social categories which flourished under the previous status quo. This pattern is constant in the history of social transformation. Because of its structuration (however loose), every resistance to change (army, social system contains mechanisms of religious power, ideology, etc.) which intervene, either to curb the process of development, or even to encourage a return to an idealized past.

However, the underdeveloped countries no longer have a choice between technological evolution and a form of civilization to which they remain attached. Their development, itself demanded by their demographic growth, must be in the direction of integration in a technological culture.

But the means of securing this integration give scope for choice. The developing countries can choose, in effect, the pattern of society or of economy which they wish to copy. While the majority of countries have not reached the stage of being able to do this, the experience of China, of Cuba, and of others, quite clearly shows us that, before being a problem of technique, development is a question of the choice of values.

2. PROBLEMS RAISED FOR THE CHURCH BY THE MUTATION OF MANKIND

As we have seen, one of the results of this permanent state of mutation in the modern world, is that groups and individuals must be able to adapt themselves continually.

Can the Church find that she too is faced with this necessity? If so, in what terms will these problems of adaptation arise for her? We shall attempt an answer to this twofold question.

In order to prolong his redemptive mission in the world, Christ has designed the Church as "structurated by apostolic power, centered upon a sacramental institution, organized in communities, and united by a charter which gives social expression to its faith and to its behavior."[1]

These characteristics constitute its very essence, and, needless to say, they do not admit of transformation.

However, in the course of time and under the inspiration of the Holy Ghost, the Church has developed institutions which enabled her to meet the needs created by her own development or connected with the changes demanded by the societies in which she found herself. Because these institutions were determined by the particular circumstance of their origin, they can be changed in later circumstances with a view to giving a better service to the Church. Now, the majority of these institutions were designed for a civilization of the pre-technical Western type. At present, they often seem to be outmoded, both in Western societies and in those into which they have been introduced with the structures of colonization. The Church may therefore be led to readjust some of her structures, and to solve problems of internal adaptation (liturgy, role of the laity, etc.) or of external adaptation (problems raised by the demographic growth, by underdevelopment, etc.).

"The Twenty-first Ecumenical Council, as Pope John XXIII emphasized, seeks to transmit in its integrity, without diminution or alternation, the Catholic doctrine which, in spite of difficulties and opposition, has grown to be the common patrimony of mankind . . . However, we hould not guard this precious treasure as though we were concerned only about the past; rather should we devote ourselves cheerfully and courageously to the work which our own era demands, thus continuing along the way which the Church has followed for close on twenty centuries.

"But the Church must also concern itself with the present time, which entails new situations and new forms of life, and which offers new opportunities for the Catholic apostolate.

"The fixed and immutable doctrines, which must be faithfully respected, should be more deeply studied and presented in a manner answering to the needs of our era. For, while the deposit of faith, i.e. the truths contained in our defined dogmas, must remain unchanged, the same is not true of the form in which these truths are presented: the form can be changed without affecting in any way the meaning and import of the doctrine. Great importance must attach to this form, and persevering work must go into its development when necessary. It should be shaped in the way best fitting a teaching of a particularly pastoral character."[8]

The signs of evangelization are also affected by the transformation of societies. What was remarked upon at one period as a collective evidence of Charity ("By this shall all men know . . .), is no longer so today. Sisters belonging to Congregations devoted to nursing and responsible for the direction and administration of hospitals, no longer constitute, in a society with a system of social security, the kind of witness to the Gospel which marked such work in the past. Their prominence is lost in the midst of similar work directed by the state. The tasks of pre-evangelization, so very important in our post-Christian era, also need to be re-defined. One cannot be in effectual touch with the world unless one keeps constantly abreast of its development.

NOTES TO CHAPTER ONE

[1]   See F. Houtart, "Faut-il revoir le dispositif apostolique," in *Un concile*

pour nôtre temps, Coll. "Rencontre," no. 62, ed. du Cerf, Paris, 1962.

[2]   From Pope John's opening discourse to Vatican Council II.

[3]   J. Frisque, "Perspectives ouvertes par la concile," in *Lettres aux communautés de la Mission de France, no.* 10, 1962, *p.*7.

[4]   See Houtart, "les Jeunes dans un monde in devenir," in *la Revue nouvelle,* 15 March 1962, p. 231. . .

[5]   In this connection, see J. Darcet, "Rapports de l'Occident avec le reste du monde," in *Prospective,* no. 3, Paris, 1959, chap. 1, 15-32.

[6]   J. Darcet, *art.cit.,* p.18.

[7]   A. Liégé, "la Mission contre les institutions chrétiennes," in *Parole et mission,* p.497.

[8]   J. Frisque, *op.cit.,* p.8.

2.
THE CONTRIBUTION
OF SOCIOLOGY
TO THE CHURCH

1. SOCIOGRAPHY OR THE DESCRIPTION OF THE PHENOMENA

The first stage in all positive research is *observation*. The observation of fact, both profane and religious, has always been a guiding factor in the Church's action. However, we are now witnessing a more systematic observation, whose technical requirements are being gradually codified. This observation is both the source and the result of sociological theory. The first observations suggest the first explicative hypotheses, which in turn are verified or discredited by further observation.

The present state of the question

In religious sociology, the efforts made during the past thirty years in Catholic milieux, have begun in most instances with a descriptive stage — in fact, with an inventory or a phenomenology of Catholicism.

Such an inventory exists for all parts of the world, and the result is a gradual improvement in our knowledge of the situation of the Church in the world.

The first step in this domain was the drawing up of statistics.

The statistical apparatus of Catholics throughout the world is being slowly perfected. Germany was the first country to carry out systematic work in this direction.[1] Spain[2] and Brazil[3] are also organized, and preliminary work is being done in Colombia,[4] Belgium and Venezuela. Some countries, such as the Netherlands and the United States,[5] have published partial statistics. We should also notice the statistics of Propaganda, those published by the *Annuaria Pontifico,* and the recent service established at the Congregation for Religious.

Up to the present, these efforts have been characterized, except over the past few years, notably in Brazil and Spain, by an inadequately developed technique and a total lack of normalization. In Italy, since the end of the last century, some statisticians have concerned themselves with religious statistics and have proposed some systems of elaboration and of calculation, but without notable success.[6] A second step consisted in establishing the description of the different exterior acts (Baptism, Sunday Mass, Communion, Marriage, Extreme Unction, etc.) and also in elaborating the statistical data and presenting them cartographically.

Gabriel Le Bras[7] and Canon Boulard[8] in France, the *Katholiek Sociaal Kerkelyk Instituut* in the Netherlands, were among the pioneers of different undertakings. Thanks to the various Institutes and Centers of socio-religious research, the majority of European countries have considerably developed their inventory.[9] In Latin America, FERES (International Federation of Catholic Institutes of socio-religious research) has done considerable work, which is in course of publication.[10] So far in the United States, little systematic work has been done in this field.[11] However, some dioceses are active, and there is, of course, *The Catholic Directory*. French Canada is beginning to publish some good studies.[12] For the most part, however, the continents of

34

Africa, Asia and Oceania have not yet been covered.

We also notice the *Bilan du Monde*,[13] the first systematic work covering every country and designed to give statistical and administrative information about the Church.

Finally, we indicate the apologetic character of these publications. The critics of the Church sometimes accuse her of being obscurantist, of being attached to an outmoded status quo; and certain Christians are beguiled into accepting such criticism. Isolated in a world of religious indifference, they may come to believe that the leaders of their Church take no account of the real outlook of the modern world. They are then tempted to voice exaggeratedly pessimistic ideas about this. The publication of exact and scientifically based data sets their minds at rest, and is irrefutable proof of Catholic concern for lucidity and truth. This form of dialogue is highly appreciated in scientific and university milieux.

Pastoral Applications

The pastoral applications of statistics and sociography in the religious field, are considerable. Let us consider this by categories of problems.

The statistics of ecclesiastical personnel have already made possible a serious tackling of the problems of distribution of manpower. In Spain, for instance, the statistical bureau of the Episcopacy has succeeded in pinpointing the number of boys prevented by lack of places from entering the minor seminaries, and also their geographical locations. The result is a ten-year plan, now approved and partly financed by the Holy See, designed to orientate these vocations towards Latin America. Again, in Brazil, the excellent statistics organization of the Brazilian Conference of Religious, makes it possible to know the qualitative and quantitative needs of each region. Thus it comes about that a considerable number of the Religious Orders and Congregations, in answer to the Pope's appeal for Latin America, are turning their attention to that region. In several other countries, notably in France, the Netherlands and Belgium, the establishment of statistics, even partial statistics, has led to changes in the distribution of the Clergy, both secular and regular.

The most decided application of sociographic studies geographically interpreted, is the disposition of religious structures: deaneries, parishes, sectors of shared pastoral work within dioceses. Methods, now highly developed, have been used to effect such dispositions, especially in towns and cities.[14] They are based on a geographico-social study of the urban milieu, a study whose purpose is to determine precisely how decanal or parochial structures should be delimited, when the population increases in a growing suburb, or when an excessively large unit has to be subdivided. Examples of the successful use of such methods can be seen, among other places, in Rotterdam, Breda, Brussels, Namur, Tournai, Lyon, Lille, Montreal, Chicago, Buenos Aires, etc.

An already solid basis on which an Episcopate at national level, and a Bishop at diocesan level, can develop certain plans, is provided by reliable statistics, by a sociographic knowledge of basic data (such as Sunday Mass attendance figures), and by the presentation of such data in graphic and cartographic forms. Diocesan examples of shared pastoral work are already multiplying. There is special evidence of this in France and in French Canada. Furthermore, we can instance, at a national level, the pastoral plan developed in Chile, and, at the international level, the decisions of the 1960 conference of CELAM bearing on pastoral care (the foundation of Institutes for pastoral care, and a Latin-American organ of socio-religious research).

Finally, we note how the enquiries instituted have rapidly produced a more acute pastoral awareness. The partitioning-off of the cultural worlds, owing to the increasing complexity of modern society, was enclosing the pastors within a too narrow area. More systematic studies alone could gradually manifest a reality which, better appreciated, in its turn effected changes in pastoral perspectives and methods of approach.

2. THE CONTRIBUTION OF SOCIOLOGY

Of great importance for theological thought is a more precise knowledge of social laws — i.e. of the major constants of life in society, for in sociology there are no absolute laws such as exist in physics. If determinism in these matters is a philosophical postulate, the social and cultural conditions are, on the other hand, a fundamental reality. Awareness of this fact led to the discovery that the field for the exercise of human freedom is often narrower than had been supposed.[15] This is one of the reasons why moral theology has, from its outset, continually expanded and clarified its positions.

Since it deals with social realities, the *social doctrine* of the Church, like all *theology concerning earthly realities,* has made considerable use of the advancements in sociology. We cannot deal with this point here, but we refer the reader to the Encyclical *Mater et magistra,* especially to the passage on socialization, and to the Encyclical *Pacem in Terris.*

On the other hand, there can today be no serious consideration of *the relations between Church and State* without reference to the development of societies. Such relations differ greatly as between a simple society and a complex society. Clearly, the transformations of the role of the State in modern nations have an effect on relations with the spiritual power.

Ecclesiology is one of the branches of theology which are now taking an increasing interest in sociology. In fact, Ecclesiology regards it as an auxiliary science. The intensification of the relations between men through the transformation of the means of communication, raises a series of new organizational problems for the Church.

It would be an error to suppose that the spread of a technological civilization in the world necessarily leads to a cultural unification of mankind. On the contrary, indeed. The shock of technological civilization makes various cultures conscious of their own identity. They are, no doubt, thrown into confusion, and no doubt some of these cultures will disappear; but, on the other hand, new and very diverse syntheses are in course of development, and this renders unitary and centralized solutions more and more illusory. From the religious viewpoint, this fact is fundamental. Now, the study of the diversity of cultural systems is engaging more and more the attention of jurists, liturgists and specialists in catechesis. They are coming to the conclusion that *neither law nor liturgy,* nor *a fortiori* cathechesis, can be uniform throughout the world. Excessive centralization, such as still exists in the Church today, can quite naturally lead to the imposing of solutions which are perfectly valid for certain regions, but much less so for other cultural milieux. Furthermore, a wide variety of pastoral situations can arise, both in missionary countries and in other parts of the world, where recourse to a central authority entails a delay which is prejudicial to the solutions urgently demanded.

No doubt, the Church preserves this centralization through concern to safeguard unity; and clearly such unity must be defended even at the price of a certain deficiency in suppleness and swiftness of adaptation. But it seems that the effective realization of this unity can equally be secured by a decentralization of administration which could go hand in hand with orientation and policy directed from the center.

The gradual creation of national and continental organs provides the intermediary structure necessary to this decentralization of responsibilities.

What is the point at issue? At the present time, the majority of problems are no longer soluble except at the national level, while many of them, because of the revolution in communication, need to be dealt with at a level far exceeding the limitations of particular State frontiers. Now, the same is true of the Church. Consider, for example, the signs of evangelization, which manifest themselves by a collective awareness of the problems of man in a modern society (underdevelopment, social injustice, technique in the service of mankind). It is difficult to have any real appreciation of such problems, merely at local or diocesan level. Again, consider the problem of vocations. There is a shortage of vocations in certain highly urbanized or industrialized dioceses, whereas more rural ones have a relatively high recruitment. Clearly, without inter-diocesan action, the problems arising from these differences will remain unsolved, thus aggravating the existing situations.

Furthermore, at the pastoral level, new services are being developed, such as liturgical, catechetical and other commissions or organs. In these domains, coordination is indispensable for the carrying out of the works undertaken and for securing the necessary economy of manpower and of means. Inter-diocesan cooperation does exist, and yet for a long time the Holy See, in its desire to guard the unity of the Church, did not favor the setting up of permanent liaison organs among the Bishops. Today, the multiplication of means of communication and of information is lessening the dangers of this formula. Almost everywhere, episcopal conferences and inter-diocesan centers are being instituted, as are also, in the case of Religious, general assemblies of the higher Superiors of the various Orders and Congregations. The present formulas are very diverse. Hence it seems indispensable to define exactly the role and the competences of these organs, if a twofold danger is to be avoided: on the one hand, their encroachment on those of the episcopal function; on the other, the paralysis of national organs. The solution would seem to be the institution of really organic and permanent episcopal conferences.

However, the national level does not exhaust the possibilities for intermediate structures. In this connection, Latin America has given a lead by the creation of CELAM (Council of Latin-American Bishops). This is a continent-scale organ of contact and coordination, having competence and power over a number of sectors. This lead has been followed by Africa, and one day, no doubt, similar measures will be taken in Asia and in Europe. The existence of large geographico-cultural groups would justify also the presence of a delegate accredited to the whole. Nothing, in fact, can measure up in importance to a diversified and comparative knowledge of the situations. At all events, and from a similar viewpoint, to develop a much more systematic knowledge of social, cultural and religious facts should be the task of a technical organ set up to collect, collate and interpret the data. Such an organ would thus provide a synthesizing basis of information. The gradual creation of national and continental organs offers the structure necessary to decentralized responsibility. Once the competences have been clearly defined, it will be sufficient to establish organic contacts with the central organs which are necessary to the functioning of the whole, and which safeguard ecclesial unity.

We should further like to indicate two other examples in a completely different domain. They concern, first of all, the study of the transformation of the social forms of human life and especially of *human communities*. Sociological analysis shows the decreasing role of the local "closed" community with meager contacts, and this is verified both in urban milieux and in technified rural millieux.

In pre-technical rural or urban societies, the majority of the social activities of the individual members were at village or district level. Whether there was question of educative, cultural, economic or religious activities, they were fulfilled by one or two basic institutions of an essentially polyvalent kind.

Such social activities have multiplied and diversified. The specialized institutions coping with these activities are established at another level. The reason is, of course, a state of affairs demanding a wider range of action; but there is also the fact of the development in communications, which eliminates the problem of distance and facilitates greater and greater mobility.

Consequently, the element of space has greatly developed in modern society. In the rural milieu, the spatial element has been broadened out to take in the region; in the urban milieu, it has extended to the whole agglomeration.

Furthermore, particularly in the urban milieu, the specialization of social institutions means, for the individual person, participation in numerous groups of monovalent character — that is, centered on a precise objective: education, leisure, work, etc. There is a wide range from which to choose, and the town or city dweller can easily change from one institution to another of the same kind.

All this implies, in the first place, a multiplication of the social roles to be fulfilled by each such dweller. The father of a family may be simultaneously a foreman, a committee member of a sports club, a member of a political party. A second consequence of this situation of multiplicity concerns the social control, i.e. the supervision, which every society exercises over its members. Whereas in a pre-technical society, global control was exercised by the fundamentally polyvalent institution, such control in modern societies becomes shared and spread, each group exercising over the individual only a partial control corresponding to the particular role which it fulfils. The global type of control is gradually disappearing; besides, it is being psychologically more and more rejected. Who would now accept, for instance, that a leisure club could exercise control over political or religious activities?

Apart from belonging to these groups, the town or city dweller uses numerous services — such as urban transport, cinemas, theaters, restaurants, supermarkets, and so forth — which exist in every sector of the social life. As the technological civilization develops, these services multiply and specialize; without them, urban life would become totally impossible. Clearly, the relations created through use of these services differ considerably according to the nature of the services themselves. They are esentially functional, and require only a superficial mutual acquaintance among their users.

A final characteristic of modern societies concerns the way in which values are established. More and more, they are transmitted in a collective manner. Values are basic to a culture, and by "culture" we mean that body of criteria for the assessment of individual and social life which a group possesses and in terms of which it organizes its collective life, defines and develops its institutions, and governs its social relationships. Quite simply, we could say that attitudes today are formed by collective transmissions.

This is perfectly logical, at least when one examines the diversified groups to which the urbanite belongs, each group having its particular role in the transmission of certain values. These specialized institutions and groups fulfil a role of the first importance, each in its own sphere; and together, these influences form a body of values which governs the social behavior-patterns of the community at large. These values are necessarily very diverse, and the development of a synthesis can only be the work of a solidly based and integrated personality. That is why, for example, the familial institution takes on such importance in the constitution of an urban society, for it is within the family that the basic personality is developed.

To this we add the means of social communication, which have multiplied at an extraordinary rate in recent decades. They have become channels for the transmission of culture and of social values. A considerable part of human knowledge is transmitted by these means, but more significant still they transmit the assessment of event and facts. They do not necessarily compete with existing institutions, notably the school, but the outcome of their multiplication is that these traditional institutions are no longer the only means which transmit values or contribute to intellectual and moral formation. Now, we are dealing with means which can reach thousands and even millions of people. They constitute a collective communication which affects each individual person and which shapes his reactions, his behavior, his attitudes. This is something fully appreciated by the political leaders of certain countries, who have transformed their method of government, thanks to the use of mass-media.

A final example may be given in connection with the findings of the demography and *sociology* of the family.[16] Just as has the progress in biological and psychological knowledge, the increased knowledge of the social environment of the family has profoundly developed the applications of moral theology, such as those concerning pastoral care and familial social action.

In a word, it is the "situation" of the world and of mankind which sociology presents to the eyes of the Church. It is not the only discipline which does this, but its role is very important. Of course, the final interpretation of man and of the human situation can be provided only by Revelation, and therefore by theology; but the materials indispensable to this interpretation will be supplied by a more precise knowledge of the realities of human life. Furthermore, the Church, the sign of God in the world, will be truly such a sign only if men perceive it to be so.

Our conclusion must be that, in the modern world, to ignore sociological findings relative to the different domains, is deliberately to shut oneself within an artificial world, or to refuse to take account of this reality created by God, on which he wills that we should act and of which he enables us to gain an ever-increasing knowledge.

The teaching of sociology and research in this science are notably in evidence in the social science faculties of Catholic universities. But it must not be overlooked that the contribution of the whole of sociology throughout the world is of great value in these matters. We shall deal later with its applications to pastoral care. We note, however, how inadequately the specific questions we speak about here are dealt with in our Catholic faculties of social sciences, whereas it is precisely in their connection that Catholics could make an original contribution to sociology, and help at the same time to make this science an auxiliary of theology. Up to the present, one must only deplore the quasi-total absence of contacts between the faculties of theology and the institutes of sociology.

3. THE CONTRIBUTION OF RELIGIOUS SOCIOLOGY

If sociology as such takes on great importance because of the materials which it supplies to the religious sciences, then the specialized branch of sociology which studies religion is of particular interest.

Since the birth of sociology, religion has provided the subject for many of its investigations. Furthermore, it is in this domain that the positivist philosophical tendency first manifested itself through an attempt at a sociological explanation of the origin of religion, the fruit of culture. It is curious that primitive religions especially have been the subject of research, and that the work of the anthropologists has often predominated. Some synthetic views have been developed about the evolution of Christianity, notably with Max Weber. However, the analysis of the Catholic and Protestant Churches is a very recent phenomenon. We may add that, generally speaking, this analysis is being done with a much more respectful attitude towards the phenomenon of religion.[17]

In religious sociology, two lines of research are in evidence, and they often combine: the study of religion in its relations with the society as a whole, and the study of religion as a social system. The first considers both the influence of religion on the social structures — as, for example, the place (or sociologically speaking, the status) of the priest in this or that society — and the importance of the religious factor in social relations and its influence on the culture (values-scale of a society).

The second aspect of the studies considers the religious institution in itself, that is as a Church or as a sect. It may then be considered as a social system, with its own structure and culture, and may be studied as such. The study of the Catholic Church will include the study of the forms of authority, that of the institutions (Religious Orders, parishes, Catholic Action), that of the Clergy and of clerical recruitment, that of liturgical assemblies regarded as social groups, that of the communications among the various organs; while the study of its cultural aspects will include the analysis of religious and moral behavior-patterns (assistance at Mass, Easter Communion, familial behavior, etc.) of religious attitudes (appreciation of the priest, for example), of pastoral care or lay apostolate in its active aspect, of the liturgy and of the catechesis as expressing cultural values, and so forth.

Having defined the field of research, we now come to the actual achievements of sociology as a science applied to pastoral care. It goes without saying that pure research, i.e. research without the immediate purpose of pastoral application, is highly important to progress in scientific knowledge. However, we are not concerned with pure research in this booklet.

Research in Religious Sociology

We have already spoken about descriptive studies regarded as sociographic. Generally speaking, the two stages — the descriptive and the sociographic — are scarcely differentiated in practice. Nearly every sociological study begins with a description or relies on statistical preliminaries. The importance of the matter obliges us to synthesize it around some major themes.

First of all, there are the studies bearing on the evolution of *the religious institution within a changing global society*. Such studies are the fruits of research into the place of religion in a technological or industrial society; or, for example, into Catholicism within North American or British or German society.[18]

Even if their application is not immediate, such works are essential to an understanding of the Church's action. We incline to the idea that they should be the object of the first efforts wherever religious sociology is being developed.

Religion *in an urban milieu* constitutes a very special subject of research. Since urbanization is one of the outstanding world phenomena, pastoral adaptation to urban life is indeed vital for the Church. After numerous descriptive studies bearing on religious structures in towns (notably parishes) and also on attitudes and behavior-patterns, a true sociological assessment of the whole matter has been inaugurated.[19]

If societies and the social behavior of individuals have developed in a certain way, we cannot expect that matters are otherwise in the religious life. It is equally evident that new problems must arise for pastoral care, the structures and activity-forms of which must therefore be re-thought. We need only instance *the institution of the parish.*

At the present time, the traditional idea of the parish remains in force. In the minds of a considerable section of the Clergy, the parish still means an autarchic religious structure based on a social group delimited by the district or village boundaries. It is by this group that the unity of Christians around the Eucharist would be assured. Now — and this is especially so in urban milieux — this basic group no longer exists, or at least is increasingly disappearing. Is it not mere illusion, therefore, to continue to act as though it existed still or could one day be restored to its original form? Why the surprise at discovering that recent investigations of Sunday Mass attendance showed more than 30 per cent of "non-parishioners" present? Why the regret at seeing "the best elements" joining movements or works outside the parochial framework? Many Christians today regard this as normal practice, and are puzzled by the criticism directed against them on this account.

Nevertheless, it is clear that such situations can create a deep uneasiness among the Clergy, an uneasiness which reveals itself in a questioning of the parochial idea itself, or in a very great difficulty in finding a pastoral answer for problems of regional or urban dimension. Quite clearly, to suppress the parish is not the answer. What should disappear is its autarchic character, for anyhow autarchy has ceased to characterize the social structures to which the parish must adapt itself. It ought to become an organic part of the higher dimension of town, city or region. This implies that certain of its functions should be re-thought and organized at the level of the new dimensions, this being especially so where a specialized apostolate (e.g. pastoral, liturgical, cate-chetical) is in question. Other functions will require the deter-mination of sectors of action and of responsibility within which several parishes will act together. Yet others will remain parochial or will be de-centralized within the parish according to the latter's size.[20]

This supra-parochial structure, an intermediary organ between the parishes and the Hierarchy, will provide an answer at a level of life where pastoral work is often non-existent, will eliminate numerous conflicts between persons responsible for religious structures, and will ensure a coordination of all the sectors of pastoral care.

However, it is not enough to regard the parish as an organic unit within a larger whole. It still remains to establish what it in fact represents in modern society.

In this connection, the work of the sociologist or psychologist is to track down, within a theological definition, the elements which must be translated into sociological or psychological terms, and to see what these terms are.

According to J. Frisque,[21] the parish is first of all the fundamental unit of the Church, because the Eucharist is celebrated within it. The specific function of the parish is, therefore, to gather baptized people together in answer to the call of God, Who, through the ministry of the priesthood — the preaching of the word and the breaking of the Bread — assures the rectitude of their faith and unifies them in charity, so that they may be to all men the sign of salvation in Jesus Christ.

This definition contains several essential elements. By way of example, we shall give some analysis of one of the essential functions of the parish: the organization of the assembly of Christians around the Eucharist.

The Assembly

How is one to define in sociological terms a Eucharistic assembly?[22] In basic sociological concepts concerning the gatherings of people, a distinction is made between a group and an aggregate. These two concepts are differentiated by the degree of interaction and of communication existing between the persons who compose them. Both words signify a gathering of people, but while a group demands a continuity in the people who compose it and reciprocal roles — as in a family, where the roles of father, of mother and of children are in constant inter-relation — an aggregate requires only physical proximity and a minimum of social relations and of communications.[23]

— *The Eucharistic assembly is sociologically defined as an aggregate and not as a group.* It requires physical proximity and social communication through conscious and active participation in a common act, but it does not demand a continuity in those

49

who constitute the assemblies. From one Sunday to another, the various assemblies in a parochial church are constituted partly by the same people and partly by others.

Nor does it presuppose an inter-relation of roles among the people who participate in the assembly. Indeed, while an awareness of forming a community is necessary, there is no formal intercommunication among all these people. In order to constitute the liturgical assembly, they need not form a group either prior or subsequent to their participation.[25]

— *The Eucharistic assembly is a specific type of aggregate with its own requirements.* There are, of course, many kinds of aggregates. There is, for example, a simple gathering of people for a temporary reason (an accident, for instance), or an audience in a cinema or theater. While these kinds can generally be lumped together into a few categories on the basis of their similarity, it indeed seems that the Eucharistic assembly constitutes a specific type which cannot be bracketed with any other.

It has two special requirements. In the first place, it must form *a community*. Here we define the constitution of a community (its objective aspect) by the creation, among its members, of an attitude of belonging (its subject aspect).[26] Now, this attitude seems to depend on two factors: on an awareness of common dependence or of solidarity; and on the active participation of each person present.[27]

It is not a matter, therefore, of a simple gathering of people who just happen to be together. Their awareness of a common dependence is a psychological attitude which can be traced to faith, but which must characterize those who constitute the Eucharistic assembly.

Add to this that one of the main qualities of an aggregate is the fact that the behavior of those who form it is collective and not social. In other words, the latter act or react together, but without interaction of roles one towards another, except sometimes to a very slight extent (when handing on the flame of the Paschal candle, for example).

However, collective behavior is not confined to an attitude of passive assistance, composed of transitory reactions, such as that of an audience at a theatre. There are other forms of collective behavior, implying an attitude of common participation in an act. This is exactly true of the Eucharistic assembly.

All this demands concrete means. In our case, it is the liturgy which defines a series of modes of collective behavior precisely in order to make concrete the sense of "togetherness," and to give it its specific significance as a common participation in one act.

In this connection, it is interesting to notice that the recent changes in the liturgy are partly in answer to a transformation of society. The elements of active participation were considerably weakened in recent centuries. They appear to have been of less consequence in a social life where, in the majority of cases, the Eucharistic assembly corresponded to a pre-existent human group (village, district). The community existed already on another basis. However, this was an ambivalent situation, for it entailed a great danger of confusion between the idea of a natural group and the idea of a supernatural one. Hence the supernatural group was liable to lose its specific nature, and to come to be regarded as merely another instance of collective behavior of the natural group.

On the other hand, with geographic dividing up of social relations and activities, a distinction appeared between the Eucharistic assembly and a pre-existent human group. The specific nature of the Eucharistic assembly is now set in relief, and should therefore be emphasized. In other words, if a real community is to be created, modes of collective behavior must be cultivated which express an active participation and which convey an awareness of solidarity in the accomplishment of the Eucharistic act.

The second requirement proper to the Eucharistic assembly is *a firm standardization*[28] *of the roles of those who preside thereat and of those who participate.* The guiding of an assembly is secured by the sacerdotal role accompanied by other auxiliary roles (deacon, reader, acolytes). These roles require a special conse- cration by the Church which establishes them all in relation with the Bishop. They are carried out according to a very precise ritual. The modes of collective behavior among the participants are also defined precisely.

We have deliberately detailed the major hypotheses which can be drawn from the many studies made of the parish unit, for we have found that the institution of the parish is one of the chief preoccupations of the pastors whom we consulted. But other sectors have been also the subject of research. We shall sum up the tendencies of the studies in progress.

The rural religious forms have not been forgotten among the subjects treated in religious sociology. The country districts are also in full evolution, with the decline in the number of farm workers, the introduction of techniques, specialization of rural centers, and increased mobility. A village is less and less a social microcosm; anyhow, it is the region which is now taking over, to become the unit of social, cultural and religious activity.

The religious roles — the secular priest, the Religious, the Nun — are also the concern of the sociologist. In the United States, an important study has been published on the priesthood as pre- senting the sociological characteristics of a profession.[29] An in- vestigation is also being made of the way in which these roles are regarded by the faithful and by non-Christians, and finally of vocations, the mode of perpetuating these roles. In this last matter, considerable progress has been made. Sociographical studies have highlighted the usual social channels of vocation (type of studies, of families, of social milieu, etc.); the social, racial or cultural beds through which these channels penetrate; and the values perceived by those who embrace this calling. Of course, these studies in no way concern the essence of the vocation, the Divine call, but deal with the social conditions for the perception of this call. However, it is not just a matter of stating such conditions; an effort must be made to examine and explain them.

We should like to give one or two examples of the type of sociological explanation offered for the observed phenomena, or in other words, to show how certain human mediations of vocation are being transformed.

— *The social significance of the priesthood changes with the passage from a rural society to an urban society.*

In the rural, pre-technical world, the role of the village priest is of very great social importance.

Besides, the priest often fulfils subsidiary roles, both directly and indirectly. His is more than a spiritual authority, and it secures for him the leadership of the community. His social status, i.e. his position in society, is high and his role is regarded as important.

As a result, becoming a priest means, in most cases, going up higher in the social scale, such ascension being not a personal matter only, but something affecting the status of the priest's family, especially in cases where he lives with some of its members.

For reasons too numerous to deal with here, the social status of the priest changes in the process of urbanization and of rural transformation. New roles come into existence to fulfil the functions formerly covered by the parish priest. If, as was the case in France with the *lois de séparation,* the State takes radical steps which affect the social status of the priest, the results of this change are very soon in evidence.

Obviously, from the viewpoint of the religious value of the sacerdotal role, this change is not necessarily bad. On the contrary, in an urbanized world, attraction towards the priesthood is for its theological value and not for its social prestige, which anyhow is no longer evident except in a few societies, such as in North America, where it is still carries a very high prestige value.

— *The changes in the status of woman in Western society is having an effect on the number of vocations.*

There is a correlation between the development of woman's role in society and the reduction of vocations to certain forms of the religious life. In present-day Western society, women are able to play an increasing number of roles. They have won political emancipation and are in process of gaining a certain degree of economic equality with men.

The situation, therefore has totally changed. In order to play a social part, especially in teaching, nursing or the social services, it is no longer necessary for a woman to enter a Religious Congregation. This is one of the elements in this situation, but there are others.

— *The transformation of the religious significance of certain social roles.*

Through the development of society, education has become one of the rights of man, assured to him by the system of compulsory education, and the system of social security makes hospitalization a similar right.

Now, this automatically means that the social roles answering to these requirements have gradually become professions, such as that of the teacher and the nurse. Since we are dealing now with professions answering to a social right, the objective witness of charity is no longer prominent in the exercise of these roles, even if charity has continued subjectively without diminution. This influences the recruitment of members for Congregations of Brothers and of Nuns, even though, from another viewpoint, it is a sign of their success. Such Congregations must gradually take on other roles and functions; for instance, they could now turn their special attention towards countries which have begun to develop.

— *Obsolete pastoral structures are one reason for the drying up of the flow of vocations.*

If young people, with the formation they have received, gather the impression that the structures of religious and pastoral action are not properly designed for their alleged purpose, the roles to be fulfilled by such structures will come to be regarded as useless.

This is often so in the case of our urban pastoral structures, but sometimes too in the case of certain Religious Congregations who are finding it difficult to adapt their forms of action to new circumstances.

Here are some examples of sociological assessment which show how important it is to discover the factors acting as secondary causes in the action of the Lord.

Up to the present time, few studies have been undertaken on Liturgy and cathechesis. The field is everywhere wide open to psycho-sociological studies and some have already been begun. It must not be forgotten, however, that these two types of religious activity cannot be separated from their general context, and that the contribution from other subjects of research forms the background fabric on which they stand in relief.

Finally, we direct attention to studies carried out in a domain which is not directly religious but which touches on numerous social and cultural activities undertaken at the Church's initiative, notably those of hospitals, schools, cooperatives, and so forth. The efficient functioning of these institutions today demands planning and constant stocktaking, and therefore calls for statistics and studies.

We cannot end this section without reference to *the institutionalization of researches*. The latter are being increasingly organized in research centers and with teams of researchers. A sociological survey of religious sociology would show that countries with a tradition of institutional Catholicism — the Netherlands (since 1946), Austria, Germany, Belgium, Great Britain — have been the first to inaugurate these centers, and that the interest aroused among responsible Religious by the works of religious sociology has gone hand in hand with efforts at pastoral renewal, in France, in the Wallonian part of Belgium, in the Netherlands, in Chile, in French Canada, in the Congo, and in certain regions of Italy, Spain, Portugal — and indeed now in the majority of countries.

In the Catholic world, two international institutions have been founded.

The first, the *Conférence internationale de sociologie religieuse,* founded in Louvain in 1946 by Canon Leclerq and with its center at Brussels, brings together those who are specializing in religious sociology. Although open to anyone actively interested in these undertakings, its primary purpose is to assist researchers by organizing periodic general meetings and conferences concerning some particular aspect of sociological theory. Its gatherings are held every three years. The 1959 sessions, for instance, held at Bologna, had as their theme, *Religion and Social Integration;* and the 1962 sessions, held at Königstein in Germany, had as theme, *The Psychological and Sociological Aspects of Membership of the Church.*

The second institution, the *Fédération internationale des Instituts de recherches sociale et socio-religieuse (FERES),* was founded at Brussels in 1958 by the countries which at that time had organized centers. Its headquarters is at Fribourg in Switzerland. It groups institutions, not persons, and has affiliated centers in the Netherlands, Germany, Great Britain, Belgium, Spain, France, Malta, Canada, Mexico, Colombia, Chile, Brazil, and the Argentine. Centers for religious statistics of Germany and Spain are Corresponding Members, and some new centers in Norway, India, Japan and the Congo have asked to be affiliated. In view of the development of activities in Latin America, a section has been created at Bogota for this continent.

An effort is also being made to promote publications. Many Catholic reviews have opened their columns to studies of religious sociology. Poly-copied notes are being circulated among themselves by sociologists of certain countries, as is the case in Italy, Belgium, France, and Norway. Finally, each of the international institutions has its particular organ. The International Conference of Religious Sociology publishes a *Bulletin de liaison,* designed for its members and giving information about developments in religious sociology; FERES, in addition to an internal bulletin, publishes *Social Compass,* the international review of socio-religious studies, which comes out six times a year. It carries articles in English and French, and aims at helping Catholic researchers at the scientific level, and at securing Catholic representation in the world of sociologists. We must also note the important scientific contribution made by the *Archives de Sociologie des Religions,* published by the *Centre national de la recherche scientifique française.*

Sociology and Pastoral Care

Pastoral Applications

It might seem that only now are we getting to the heart of our subject, but in reality it only remains to draw our conclusions. The concrete areas of pastoral application are already numerous, and we cannot possibly list them all here.

— The Pastoral structures

Established structures always offer a certain resistance to change, and cannot be expected to adapt themselves very quickly. We have already referred to this in connection with the application of sociographical researches.

The geographical distribution of the Clergy and even of certain sacerdotal tasks has been studied, for example, in the diocese of Namur, in some dioceses of the Netherlands, in the Belgian provinces of the Dominicans, in the destination of priests sent to Latin America by the Spanish Hierarchy, at the *Mission de France,* and so forth.

— Pastoral Action

Thanks to the spread of an improved general understanding of pastoral necessities in a changing world, and also in consequence of particular studies, pastoral action is gradually being transformed.

This is especially noticeable in urban milieux. The discovery of the town in all its dimensions, leads to a complete re-thinking of its pastoral pattern. Investigation is required, both into structures and into practical approaches, for we are still too involved in a pastoral pattern of the rural kind. However, little by little we shall discover the forms which urban pastoral care should take. This discovery is coming about thanks both to research and to pastoral experience. In towns and cities where the two work together, tangible progress is being made.

Some experiments would be worth a detailed account — for example, those of Rotterdam, of Bologna, of Bogota, and of some French towns. It is clearly the whole pattern of pastoral care which is being gradually tackled in such experiments.

The present demands of missionary pastoral care could supply another example. Several studies of this question are in preparation, notably in Belgium, at the request of the clergy. What are the places where the preaching of the message of salvation no longer exists? How can such missions be re-established? Apart from religious requirements, what are the sociological dimensions of missionary pastoral work?

There are also many possible applications in the rural world, and these have been most in evidence in France. We have already referred to some structures and to the re-distribution of the Clergy as a result of sociographical studies, and we may add that nearly every diocese which has redistributed its territory in pastoral zones has also transformed its practical approaches.

Reference must also be made to the work done by the regional missions, work which is often based on a sociological study whose value varies from place to place. Finally, there is the pastoral influence of men such as Canon Boulard and Father Motte, not only in France but also in Africa and in the three Americas, an influence which results, of course, from their experience, but which can also be traced to the researches and studies they have carried out.

To end this very incomplete enumeration, we must refer in general to the immense work done by the anthropologists and ethnographers, especially in Africa, Asia, Oceania and Latin America, the latter being an example on the continental scale.[30]

If the Latin American continent is in full development, it is nevertheless encountering the difficulties incident to rapid evolution: extraordinary demographic growth, unbalanced economic expansion, unstable political systems, outmoded social structures, confused cultural values. In fact, the problem of Latin America is essentially posed in terms of social change, change affecting all the elements of life in society both at the level of its organization and at that of its cultural values.

It is readily understood, therefore, that the Church in Latin America must face up to a new situation which will develop even more rapidly in the years ahead. There is every indication that, in the period 1960-2000, there will be a demographic increase of 400 millions. Furthermore, in a few years hence there will be a very changed world, much more literate and urbanized, and, thanks to mass-media, sharing a uniformly world-wide culture.

The Latin American Church is faced, therefore, with a missionary task in the full sense — no less than the evangelization of a 400 millions increase of population in a new society and a new culture which require to be orientated by Christian values. Whereas in a relatively stable society it was sufficient to carry out a pastoral program aimed at conserving faith, we are now entering into a new era which demands a dynamic pastoral approach.

From the religious viewpoint, the social change entails, in Latin America, both quantitative and qualitative consequences.

QUANTITATIVE CONSEQUENCES

— *Number of inhabitants per priest*

At present, there is an estimated number of about 5,300 people per priest. This number reveals a situation made more difficult by the fact that it urgently demands a short term pastoral policy of an essentially dynamic type. Now, it is highly improbable that the future, on present indications, will bring an improvement. Forecasts based on calculations of population increase, of sacerdotal manpower and of vocations, indicate a gradual increase in the number of inhabitants per priest. By the end of the century, the proportion could be one priest to 7,400 people.

— *Dimension of parochial structures*

While the average size of parishes is about 992 km^2 and the average number of parishioners is 15,332, it is a fact, however, that these averages are very considerably exceeded in 134 (out of 348) parishes. In the big towns, the population of certain parishes can reach 50, 80 or even 100 thousand inhabitants. Quite clearly, such structures can guarantee an effective religious ministry only for a limited number of the people.

— *The Sacraments*

Although the vast majority of the population (more than 90 per cent) are baptized into the Catholic Church, the reception of the other sacraments is often impossible in practice because of the shortage of priests and the inadequacy of the parochial structures. Certain studies have shown that, in Peru and Venezuela, for example, 3 to 5 per cent of the rural population received weekly pastoral services. In the towns, religious practice varies between 10 and 20 per cent. Participation in the Eucharist is therefore confined to a minority. As for the sacrament of Penance and the sacrament of the Sick, these do not exist in practice for the vast majority of the Latin American peoples.

— *Sects and Spiritualism*

The sects are making considerable progress. During the past 25 years, the proportion of Protestants (sects and churches) has risen from 0.49 to 3.84 per cent. In Brazil, Spiritualism is also making headway. Analysis of the causes for this advance shows, on the one hand, a failure to find in the very formal structures of Catholicism (excessively large parishes) satisfaction of inner spiritual and religious needs; and, on the other, the psycho-social shock which is due to the overthrow of the social structures.

The Latin American Church has certainly not remained insensible to this situation. Its efforts have been directed especially to promoting vocations, to multiplying pastoral structures, and to developing catechesis. Nevertheless, such efforts are not yet sufficient to solve the problem of the evangelization of the masses, both urban and rural. *Urgent* solutions are necessary if the Church is not to be left far behind by change and growth. Among such solutions, the fundamental move would seem to be the decentralization of pastoral action. Now, if the number of priests is insufficient to meet this decentralization, the clear conclusion is that others must be called upon to assist. Religious not in Holy Orders and also Nuns could certainly be of valuable help to the Clergy. Furthermore, the establishment of many more religious houses in rural regions should be envisaged. The magnitude of the undertaking and the gravity of the situation are such, however, that pastoral decentralization cannot be effected unless certain religious functions in the service of the Christian community are entrusted to laymen. Already in certain regions, the preaching of the word and catechetical work are left to them. But there could and must be a multiplication of prayer-meetings directed by laymen, such as already exist in Africa and Asia, and this could eventually lead to their being permitted to distribute certain sacraments (Baptism, the Eucharist, Matrimony). Of course, this move could not be made without strict rules and without vigilant control by the Bishop, but the multiplication of dioceses and the improvement in the means of communication have greatly facilitated the possibility of a mission of this kind in Latin America.

QUALITATIVE CONSEQUENCES

It can be said that the majority of the people of Latin America have the Faith and that they express it through attachment to Catholicism. The transmission of religious values implied by this has been made possible, despite the shortage of priests, because of the type of society in which the majority of the population were living — a society of the traditional rural type characterized by social immobility and by marginality. As a result of this pattern, the currents of ideas which were making themselves felt in the towns, and the anti-religious political régimes, had relatively little influence on the rural masses. Today, however, the demographic growth and the perfecting of the means of communication, both geographical and ideological, are deeply transforming the rural society which is becoming increasingly impregnated with a technological civilization and with its values. The social structures (and more especially the patriarchal-type family), which ensured the transmission of cultural values (including religious values), are in full course of change and even on their way to extinction. Henceforward, a quasi-natural transmission of these values cannot be expected. On the other hand, the new social forms coming into existence are often linked up with scales of values (capitalist or marxist) in conflict with Christianity, and are therefore becoming nuclei of de-christianization. Hence this twofold consequence of social change necessitates a new pastoral approach which must be thought out along theological, sociological and psychological lines.

Furthermore, the Church must rapidly create its own instruments of transmission. Accordingly, one can assess the fundamental importance of catechesis. The development of the latter raises more than organizational problems; its content must be considered in terms of the masses to whom it is addressed, masses whose religious type is still very close to nature and therefore to a cosmic religion. Use of the mass-media of communication (press, radio, T.V.) will contribute to the solution.

Moreover, when there is a perfect equation between membership of a natural group (family, village, nation) and membership of a religious group, there is clearly a danger that religion comes to be regarded as a simple service of society. The linkage is such that a change in the type of society may automatically involve the disappearance of the religious membership. One of the principal aims of a dynamic pastoral program, therefore, will be to foster a sense of belonging to the Church. Supernatural membership of the Mystical Body of Christ is, of course, assured by Baptism, but this is not sufficient to create a living awareness of forming part of a social body having a visible form. This sense of belonging can be given only by a real participation, either of a popular kind (processions, pilgrimages, whose content and expression must be given a new form) or of a more developed kind (liturgical renewal, lay apostolate). The decentralization of pastoral action plays an important part in this domain.

Finally, in the change from one type of society to another, there are key points at which are being developed not only the structures of the society of tomorrow but also its values. In Latin America, such points are the universities, the workers' movements, the nascent peasant organizations, and so forth. Intensive action, concentrating manpower and means, should be directed at these sectors, even if this involves the temporary neglect of other sectors. This clearly presupposes a common pastoral policy and attitude going beyond the limits, not only of individual parishes, but also of individual dioceses.

PRE-EVANGELIZATION

Social change affects the Church not only as an institution, for its relations with lay society are also equally transformed. The social presence of the Church can no longer be assured by elements of exterior magnificence; that presence can now be assured only by the Church's clear preoccupation with the fate of men suddenly launched on an enormous adventure, by its efficacious love of the poor, and by its contribution to the integration of society and of values.

The action of the Church in this domain may be exercised more particularly in certain directions.

In the first place, a theology of temporal things ought to be developed in terms of the concrete problems of the continent. Up to now, the accepted doctrinal attitude regarded the temporal world as a simple instrument of the spiritual society, and often ignored the fact that God has given mankind the mission to develop the earth. One of the results of this was the formation of a lay élite, very fervent it is true, but cultivating a detachment from the lay world. In a continent where the fundamental human problem is economic, social and cultural development, this fact entails serious consequences.

Furthermore, the role of the hierarchy is to guide Christians in their moral judgments, and therefore to orientate their conduct. Among other things, this mission implies the taking up of definite positions in certain domains: basic agrarian, fiscal, educational, administrative reforms aimed at removing obstacles to development, etc.

The involvement of the laity in the social revolution will be an even more important sign of the Church's presence. It will express in a concrete way the charity of Christ towards men *as men,* and it can never become a nucleus or a manifestation of power.

But such an involvement entails major consequences for the work of evangelization. The latter will consist in creating a community of faith, of worship and of charity with *these* men, and not with an élite who are marginal to a developing world.

We have taken Latin America as an example, the better to clarify the importance which sociological knowledge has in relation to pastoral policy and care.

NOTES TO CHAPTER TWO

[1]   *Katholischer Handbuch,* Koln, regularly published since 1920.

[2]   *Guia de la Iglesia de España,* Oficina de estadisticas de la Iglesia, Madrid.

[3]   *Annuario dos religiosos do Brasil,* Conferencia dos religiosos do Brasil, Rio de Janeiro.

[4]   *Annuario cattolico de Colombia,* published by the Centro de investigaciones sociales, Bogota.

[5]   *Catholic Directory,* P. J. Kenedy and Sons, New York.

[6]   G. BERTOLOTTI, *Statistica ecclesiastica d'Italia,* Savona, 1885. This work began a tradition which was to be continued by G. de Rossi, "Cio che possomo dire i dati statistici di una parrochia" in *Vita e Pensiero,* t. 1, 1914-1915, p.289 -300, by P. Corti, S.J., "l'Apostolato dell'Azione Cattolica, perchè gli uomini vivano in grazia di Dio," in *Ut vitam habeant,* Rome, 1935; by A. Canaletti-Gaudenti, "De Statistico Officio in Ecclesiae usum constituendo," in *Apolinaris,* t.9, 1936, p.85-111; by F. Brambilla, S.J., "Realtà di anime e metodi di apostolado," in *Civiltà cattolica,* July-August 1943, p. 96-102, 261-269, and by the contemporary works and articles by Don Leoni, G. Burgalassi, F. Acquaviva, etc. In Germany, since the beginning of the century, a similar position was made: H. Krose, S.J., "Zur Frage der Einrichtung eines Büros für katholische Statistik," in *Histor.polit.Blätter,* T.134, 1904, p.830 ss.

[7]   G. Le Bras, *Introduction a l'histoire de la pratique religieuse en France,* 2 vol., Paris, 1942 et 1945.

[8]   F. Boulard, *Problèmes missionaires de la France rurale,* 2 vol., Ed. du Cerf, Paris, 1945.

Sociology and Pastoral Care

[9] In France, there have been numerous works concerning religious practice. Here is a selected list of investigations on a diocese or region: *Diocèse d'Annecy, Album de sociologie religieuse,* 1956-1957, Annecy 1958. — *la Pratique dominicale dens les zones urbaines de Saôneet-Loire,* Autun, Direction des Oeuvres, 3 fasc., 1957-1958. — *Visages de l'Oise,* s.l.n.d., 1958. — *Sociologie et pastorale, Diocèse de Coutances,* Éd. Notre-Dame, 1957. — *Recherches pastorales,* 1957, Canton de Fribourg, Suisse, Centres d'études pastorales, Grand Séminaire, 1958. — *la Haute-Marne, le diocèse de Langres,* Évêché de Langres, 1960. — *Sociologie et pastorale, Diocèse de Poitiers,* Poitiers, s.d., 1959. — *Finistère,* 1958, t.1: *Aspects humains et economiques,* t.11: *Aspects religieux,* Quimper, Secrétariat social, 2 vol. 1960. — S. Ligier, *Recherches sociologiques sur la pratique religieuse du Jura,* 4 fasc., 1951. — *Pratique religieuse et orientations pastorales, Diocèse de Séez,* Alençon, Direction des Oeuvres, 1956. — *Sociologie et pastorale, Diocèse de Viviers,* s.1., 1958.; L. Gros, *la Pratique religieuse dans le diocèse de Marseille,* Paris, Éd. Ouvrières, 12, avenue Soeur-Rosalie, Paris, 13e, 1953. — *le Recensement de pratique religieuse dans la Seine,* 14 March 1954, Paris, I.N.S.E.E., 29, quai Branly, Paris 7e, 1958. — *le Diocèse de Versailles, Sondages historiques, recensement de pratique religieuse de 1954. Conclusions pastorales,* Versailles, Évêché, 1959. — R. P. Marie-André, *Documents de Pastorale,* Toulouse 1957. — Jean Labbens and Roger Daille, *la pratique dominicale dans l'agglomeration lyonnaise,* 3 fasc., Institut de Sociologie, 25, rue du Plat, Lyon, 1955-1957. — *Diocèse de Nice, la Pratique dominicale, Enquête de sociologie religieuse,* 1954, Nice, Direction des Oeuvres, 1959. — Jean Verscheure, *Premiers Aspects de l'enquête du 23 octobre 1955 à Lille, sur la pratique- messe, le dimanche, des 12 ans et plus,* Lille, Centre diocésain d'études socio-religieuses, 39, rue de la Monnaie, 1956. — Paul Gouyon, *la Pratique religieuse de l'agglomération bordelaise, essai de pastorale,* Bordeaux, Librairie "les bons livres" et Maison des Oeuvres 1957. — On the method to be used to secure these recensions, see specially Jean Labbens, *les 99 autres,* Vitte, Paris-Lyon, 1954, et Centre catholique de sociologie religieuse: *Comment réaliser un recensement d'assistance à la messe dominicale,* Fleurus, Paris, 1960; J. Versheure, *Aspects sociologiques de la pratique dominicale. Diocèse de Lille,* Centre diocésain de recherches socio-religieuses, Lille, 1961.

Here are some examples from other countries: Netherlands: the numerous reports of the *Katholiek Sociaal Kerkelijk Instituut.* — Italy: Studies of the dioceses of Mantua and of Volterra and especially the recent works by Don A. Toldo on the practice of religion in the deanerie of Barrano,

Monte San Pietro, Savigno, Loiano and of Vado, published by the Centre diocésain de recherches socio-religieuses in 1960 and 1961. — Austria: Studies on the practice of religion in the deaneries of many towns, notably Linz, Innsbruck, Vienna, etc., of l'I.K.I.K.S. or Centre of Socio-religious Research. — Belgium: Many reports from *Centre de recherches socio-religieuse* of Brussels, notably on Brussels, Tournai, Mons, Namur, Gand, Liège, Charleroi, Seraing, the Diocese of Bruges and many rural deaneries. — Switzerland: Various investigations have been assembled in one volume by Father Pilloud on *la Pratique religieuse de la Suisse Romande*. — Spain: Studies of Barcelona, Madrid, etc., notably by Father Duocastella. — Great Britain: Various statistical studies have been made by the *Demographic Survey* of the Newman Association. (We must also indicate the works done in Portugal, Luxembourg, Malta, Norway and Poland, especially the works of the Catholic University of Lublin and the investigation carried out on Warsaw).

[10]   The researches undertaken in 1958, initiated by Mgr. L.-G. Ligutti, thanks to the help of the "Homeland Foundation" and under my direction, were published in Spanish by FERES.

[11]   C.-J. Nuesse and T.-J. Harte, *c. ss. r.*, *The Sociology of the Parish*, Milwaukee, 1951; G. J. Schnepp, *Leakage from a Catholic parish*, C. U. of A. Washington, D.C., 1942; J. H. Fichter, *s.j.*, *Southern Parish*, vol. 1, *The Dynamics of a City Church*, Chicago, 1951; F. Houtart, *Aspects sociologiques du catholicisme americain*, Éd. Ouvrières, Paris, 1958; W.-T. Liu, *The Marginal Catholics in the South. A revision of concepts*, in *American Journal of Sociology*, vol.LXV, no. 4, 1960, p.383-390.

[12]   Studies have been made, notably on the dioceses of *Saint-Jean*, of *Saint-Jérôme*, of *Sainte-Anne-de-la-Pocatière* and of *Québec*. Others are in preparation at Montreal and Chicoutimi.

[13]   *Bilan du Monde, Encyclopédie catholique du monde chrétien*, 2 vol., Casterman, Tournai-Paris, 1958 and 1960.

[14]   See especially works by A. Sokolski, in *Paroisses urbaines et paroisses rurales*, Casterman, 1958 and in the review, *Social Compass*.

[15]   J. Leclercq, *op. cit.*

[16]   J. Delcourt, *Famille et civilisation urbaine*, la Pensée catholique, Brussels, 1960.

[17]   We have especially in mind the following: J. Wach, *Einführung in die Religions soziologie*, Möhr, Tübingen, 1935; (translated into English and later supplemented as *Sociology of Religion*); G. Mensching, *Soziologie der Religion*, L. Rohnscheid Verlag, Bonn, 1947: M. Yinger, *Religion, Society and the Individual*, Macmillan, New York, 1957.

Sociology and Pastoral Care

[18] F. Houtart, *Aspects sociologiques du catholicism americain,* ed. Ouvrières, Paris, 1958.

[19] There are now many studies on this subject. Apart from those already indicated, there are: J.-H. Fichter, *Social relations in the urban Parish,* Univ. of Chicago Press, 1954; J. Labbens, *l'Église et les centres urbains,* Spès, Paris, 1959; F. Houtart "Dimensions nouvelles de la paroisse urbaine," in *Nouvelle Revue théologique,* April 1958, p.384 ss.; "L'aménagement religieux des territoires urbains," in *la Revue nouvelle,* December, 1958, p.517 ss; "les Conditions sociales de la pastorale dans les grandes villes," in *Social Compass,* 1959, p. 181 ss.; *la Mentalidad religiosa en las grandes ciudades,* Univ. of Bogota, 1959; "Grosstadtpastoration" in *Scheitzer Rundschau,* February, 1957, p.639 ss.; E. Pin, "Can the Urban Parish be a Community?" in *Gregorianum,* XLI, no. 3, 1960, p.393 ss.

[20] See F. Houtart, "les Structures de l'Église," in *Qu'attendons-nous du concile?,* la Pensée catholique, Brussels, 1960.

[21] J. Frisque, "Pour une théologie des rapports entre la mission et la paroisse," in *la Revue nouvelle,* 18e année, t.XXXV, no. 6, 15 June, 1962, p.579-592.

[22] See F. Houtart, "Note sur la sociologie de la paroisse comme assemblée eucharistique," in *Social Compass,* vol. X, no 1, 1963.

[23] J. Fichter, S.J., *Sociologie,* Éd. Universitaires, Brussels, 1960, p.90.

[24] The term *aggregate* is used in its sociological sense and does not imply a judgment of value. It signifies a particular form of human gathering which is neither better nor less good than a *group.*

[25] One might ask whether the Eucharistic assembly does not rather form a public; but, according to J. Fichter, the concept *public* does not necessarily imply the physical proximity which is required in the case we are considering.

[26] Here I follow E. Pin, S.J., *Sociologie de la paroisse,* p.7 (notes).

[27] *Ibidem.*

[28] The word "standardization" is not used here with the pejorative sense sometimes attaching to it. It simply signifies that the acts are done according to a very strictly established model.

[29] J. H. Fichter, *Religion as an Occupation,* University of Notre Dame Press, 1956. The bibliography on this question in *Social Compass,* vol.III, no 4, 1961, may also be consulted.

[30] F. Houtart, *l'Église latino-americaine à l'heure du Concile,* Feres, Fribourg, 1963.

CONCLUSIONS

All this leads on to two conclusions: that the province of sociology has a more general context, demanding organic contacts with other disciplines — with demography, psychology, anthropology; and that sociology is a discipline necessary to pastoral care.

It must be admitted, however, that as yet sociology has met with difficulties in answering the immediate preoccupations of the pastors. What emerges throughout the present work is that what sociology especially contributes is material for intermediate and long term assessment.

Gradually, however, sociology is also getting round to short term perspectives. At the outset, indeed, religious sociology came into existence in Catholic milieux in order to be of service to pastoral care, the idea having originated with the pastors and not with the sociologists; but the resultant initial works have been quickly outpassed for they were principally sociographical studies giving a more precise description of the situation of each parish dealt with.

At first, their findings constituted a real discovery through the precise information they supplied about the degree of religious practice in the various parishes, the influence of the class system on religious practice (numerical, at least), the pattern of Baptisms, of the Sacraments, etc.

Today, such findings are common knowledge, especially with priests. If a priest now sets up a survey of religious practice in his parish and discovers that the middle class contains more practising Catholics than does the working class, he is not learning something he did not already know.

The exact knowledge supplied by research undertakings is not, of course, useless, but of what value is it to pastoral policy to know whether the figure of practising working class parishioners is 11.25 or 13.75 per cent?

Hence it is that one senses a certain disappointment and even a certain boredom with studies of religious practice at the local level.

Moreover, parish priests have also come to regard rather sceptically the studies carried out at the regional level. They cannot see what application can possibly be made of their findings at the local level.

Have we not reached, therefore, a critical moment in religious sociology as applied to pastoral care? This is what many are asking themselves, and some have already anwered the question by saying that sociology can no longer add anything really new.

The fundamental requirement is that we must get away from the monograph tradition. Of course, certain fundamental data about parochial life should be gathered: religious practice, in so far as it can be a significant item, especially when the investigation is directed to a single parish, in view of the mobility of Mass attenders; reception of the different sacraments; the constitution of the parish nucleus, etc. All this is good, and every parish priest ought to have a permanent dossier of the basic data of his parish.

At the same time, such a dossier still tells him nothing about the solutions which he must find in his pastoral work. Very often, priests who sought a sociological survey were expecting to receive something quite other than a simple description. They supposed, perhaps unconsciously, that the description would immediately show them what should be done. But the sociological survey does nothing of the kind. It must be admitted, however, that many "religious sociologists" have fallen into the same trap.

In sociology, the answer does not come with merely a more precise knowledge of the facts; a knowledge of the procedures and of the causes is also needed. Hence the necessity for going beyond the purely descriptive to a deeper sociology. That is why there can be no religious sociology without sociology pure and simple.

But the scientific method still requires a supplementary measure. If research is to result in action, then definite objectives must be decided in advance.

When a parish priest seeks a survey of his parish, e.g. in order to prepare for a mission, it is no good to present him with a splendid monographic description of the parish.

The first step is to determine, with the parish priest or the parochial clergy, what are to be the objectives of the mission. It is only when this has been settled, with the help of the sociologist, that the plan of study can be drawn up.

Surveys and researches must, therefore, be narrowed to specific objectives. Let us suppose the primacy objective decided upon for the proposed mission to be the "awakening of a Christian group to a more "community" attitude at the liturgical level. Once this has been settled, work can begin by asking those who use the Church to answer a certain number of questions directly concerning the liturgy. This will serve to reveal what thoughts they have on this subject, how they react, what their wishes are in the matter, and from all this it will be possible to deduce the obstacles which eventual change will encounter. This, in turn, will make it possible to develop certain plans (sermons, etc.) designed to foster a "community" attitude towards the liturgy.

Suppose, on the other hand, that the precise object decided on for the mission is an attempt to make the parish nucleus (committee, etc.) more apostolic, the survey will be directed accordingly. First, all the information will be gathered which is necessary to an acqaintance with the nucleus, in its dimensions of age, of sex, of profession. Next, the enquiry will center on the members themselves to find out, for example, how close is their connection with the group, with the parish or more generally with the Church, how they regard other groups, what their attitude is towards choices of missionary works, etc. On the results obtained, a program can then be drawn up aimed directly at rendering the group more apostolic.

Again, if the objective proposed for the mission is the influencing of a particular category of the lapsed or even of non-believers, the survey will be finally orientated towards this objective.

All this shows how important it is that the objectives should be clear and limited, both as to time and space. One cannot take, even as the objective of a mission, the conversion of all the parishioners. To be really efficacious, a mission must be a limited one.

It can be seen, therefore, that religious sociology is still able to assist the clergy, even at the local level. It would be wrong to become discouraged in pastoral action because the problems today are in totally different terms, and because neither all the structures nor all the forms of action adapted to the present situation have been found. Similarly, it would be a mistake to adopt a negative attitude towards the contribution which sociology can make to pastoral work, on the pretext that this contribution contains nothing really new. A fresh stage should be inaugurated, which would enable the sociologist to play a new role in much closer contact with pastoral work.

Hence it is important, in every diocese or region which has courageously inaugurated an effort at pastoral renewal, that there should be some qualified person (priest or layman) appointed to collaborate in this work. Everyone would agree that a theology which really sets out to orientate pastoral care, demands theologians who are actually involved in this care, and surely it should be regarded as equally necessary that sociologists should play a part in pastoral action.

This is not a matter of personal taste or of fashion; it is a concern to continue a long tradition of the Church by using the means at hand. Knowledge of the human condition demands today a method adapted to its complexity, and we know that such knowledge has always been one of the foundations of the art of pastoral care. Fidelity to the Lord requires that we should hear his word, both in the Scriptures and in the realities of life.[1]

NOTE

[1] Two works by Catholics on religious sociology have been published which deal particularly with its applications to the study of Catholicism. They are: J. LABBENS, *La Sociologie religieuse,* Fayard, Paris, 1959; and W. Goddijn and H. P. Godijn, *Godsdienst-sociologie,* Het Spectrum, Utrecht, 1959. The second work has been translated into German.